THE Survival Guide for Young Catholics

John Chater

Published by Redemptorist Publications
Alphonsus House, Chawton, Hampshire, GU34 3HQ, UK
Tel. +44 (0)1420 88222 Fax. +44 (0)1420 88805
Email: rp@rpbooks.co.uk
Website: www.rpbooks.co.uk

A registered charity limited by guarantee
Registered in England 3261721

Editors: Lisa Gregoire and Christine Clark
Designer: Nuttifox

ISBN 978-0-85231-424-1

A CIP catalogue record for this book is available from the British Library.

Nihil Obstat: Rev. William Wilson
              Censor deputatis
Imprimatur: + Rt. Rev. Philip A. Egan BA, STL, PhD
              Bishop of Portsmouth
              27th January 2015

The *Nihil Obstat* and *Imprimatur* are official declarations that a book or pamphlet is free of doctrinal or moral error. No implication is contained therein that those who have granted the *Nihil Obstat* and *Imprimatur* agree with the contents, opinions or statements expressed.

The publisher gratefully acknowledges permission to use the following copyright material:

Fr Andrew Pinsent and Fr Marcus Holden: *Lumen: The Catholic Gift to Civilisation* (London: LTS, 2011); photos: page 35: Waiting for the Word, Foter; page 55: GlasgowAmateur, Foter and caddy_corner, Foter; page 79: "Conflict", metal, 30cm x 10cm x 30cm, by Yiannis Dendrinos; the prayers on pages 97-100, which were written by Jack Regan.

Excerpts from *The Jerusalem Bible*, copyright © 1966 by Darton, Longman & Todd, Ltd and Doubleday, a division of Random House, Inc. Reprinted by permission.

Printed by Portland Print, Kettering, NN16 8UN

About the author

Who wrote *The Survival Guide for Young Catholics*? I did, but not alone. As a middle-aged man, a book just written by me for young people would be of limited interest to its intended audience. Fortunately, through various Catholic youth and confirmation groups, I know many young Catholics who have been willing to discuss the themes of this book and to share their ideas with me.

At this point it is probably worth mentioning my own expertise in the field of theology ("God studies"), setting out why it is that I am qualified to write a book like this. Unfortunately this is difficult to do because I'm not an expert in anything in particular. I am just like you. I was baptised a Catholic and have, for a number of years, tried to come to an amateur's understanding of what Catholicism is and why it speaks more truthfully than any of the alternatives that I've considered.

So I am not speaking to you from "on high" as it were, but rather I am sitting next to you in the pews, sharing the same feelings of uncertainty and trying to make sense of something that at times may seem like nonsense.

John Chater

To the memory of the Rt Rev Michael Evans, Fr Vincent Miceli SJ and Fr Hugh Thwaites SJ, and also to the memory of my father, Derek Chater.

Acknowledgements

With gratitude to Canon Peter Stodart, Vittoria Williams, Michele Youatt and the many young Catholics who join us each year for the confirmation programme at St Augustine's Church in Tunbridge Wells, from where the idea of this book arose.

I am especially indebted to Canon John Redford and Fr Marcus Holden for reviewing and improving the text and to Max Chater for advising on original content.

Finally, I would like to acknowledge my mother who taught me not to take anything for granted and to question everything – especially my faith.

Contents

Foreword

After twenty-three long and exhausting hours of travel and a brief stop in Singapore and Dubai, we finally made it to Sydney, Australia for World Youth Day 2008. Although slightly tired I was struck by the crowds and the colour that filled the place as young people from all over the world poured into the airport. Curiosity and excitement was definitely in the air. I vividly remember that as we walked to our coach I caught sight of an American group finishing prayers and making the sign of the cross. At that moment I was reminded and inspired that all the colour, crowds, noise and excitement was for the celebration of our common belief that we are all united in faith. This was the beginning of a discovery that is still taking place to this day in my life. To be Catholic is, as St John Paul II said, "a noble and authentic adventure". It is the adventure we were made for.

Anybody who has ever been to World Youth Day would appreciate that in those two weeks it's easy to be a Catholic – you have so much fun spending days learning and discovering the beauty of your faith, and you share and celebrate what it means to be Catholic. Unfortunately, the daily reality for us young Catholics here in the UK is quite different. Instead of being surrounded by the colours and flags of a supportive crowd, we are surrounded by sceptics, critics and those unsympathetic to our faith. We are often asked: "Why do you go to church anyway?" "Do you actually believe in God?" These questions are usually posed as though our faith is some childish practice, equivalent to believing in Father Christmas or the tooth fairy.

We also get challenged on its morals and values, with some people believing that Catholics are homophobic and against women's rights and equalities – how far from the truth! It's not only the things said. It can often be the looks of disapproval or prejudice faced in the workplace, or in school, when we do decide to step out in faith.

I remember one example when I was standing in the middle of a Freshers' Fair giving flyers to

people and starting small talk with students about the Catholic Society. I approached one guy who was standing close by. He immediately warned me that he was not interested. Keen to know why he seemed so against the Catholic faith I asked him to explain where he was coming from. Mistake! The onslaught began, the conversation turned into an attack, and the attack felt personal and full of anger. Following Jesus was never going to be easy and this book may not have a magical solution to making it easy.

In 2010 I had the privilege of meeting Pope Benedict XVI with two and a half thousand other young Catholics who were vocal and vibrant about their faith. I was asked to welcome the Pope on behalf of young people. It was a truly life-changing and powerful encounter, and from his gentle frame came words of challenge and encouragement for each of us.

Humorously, but seriously, he said: "Christ did not promise an easy life. Those who desire comforts have dialled the wrong number. Rather, he shows us the way to great things." In other words, we are made for greatness and not for comfort. If we choose comfort we forfeit greatness; and if we choose greatness then, to some extent, we forfeit comfort. So it's not about making it easy and settling for second best. It's about equipping ourselves and striving to be all that we can and should be. We need to know our faith to own our faith, and through this conviction we should come to love it so that we can really live it.

I believe *The Survival Guide for Young Catholics* will help to equip us – not only to survive, but to thrive, confident that God loves us and desires us to live out our lives and our faith to the full.

Paschal Uche *was selected amongst many young Catholics in Britain to welcome Pope Benedict XVI to the UK in 2010.*

Introduction

"To know much and taste nothing – of what use is that?"

St Bonaventure

Introduction

Catholicism is a religion that has produced some of the most outstanding and original thinkers – men and women who have questioned every aspect of their faith, testing it to breaking point in their search for understanding. They have also stood at the forefront of knowledge in science, literature, art, music and medicine. They did not blindly accept what they were told, so why should you?

Seven outstanding Catholic thinkers

1. Leonardo da Vinci (1452 – 1519)
Considered one of the greatest painters of all time

2. Georges Lemaître (1894 – 1966)
Father of the Big Bang theory

3. Mother Teresa (1910 – 1997)
A nun whose charity work earned her a Nobel Peace Prize

4. J. R. R. Tolkien (1892 – 1973)
Popularly identified as the "father" of modern high fantasy literature

5. René Descartes (1596 – 1650)
One of the key thinkers of the Scientific Revolution in the Western world

6. Thomas Aquinas (1225 – 1274)
An immensely influential philosopher and theologian in the tradition of scholasticism

7. Irena Sendler (1910 – 2008)
A social worker who defied the Nazis to save the lives of some two thousand five hundred Jewish children in the Warsaw Ghetto during the Second World War

What is this book about?

The aim of this book is to help you to deal with some of the many arguments against your faith that you are bound to encounter – if you haven't already. You can also use it to "pressure test" Catholicism, to see if it stands up to criticism. This will help you to decide whether or not your faith is reasonable, logical and worthy of your lifelong devotion.

Primarily *The Survival Guide for Young Catholics* is aimed at Catholics or those interested in Catholicism within the age range of fourteen to twenty. It may also be of interest to teachers, catechists, or anyone who wants to learn about some of the things that make faith challenging for the current and future generations of Catholics.

What it is not, however, is a book that seeks to "convert". Conversion, if it comes, can only come from within a person – it cannot be driven from the outside. Christians believe that faith is a gift, which must be willingly accepted. If, after reading this book, you feel convinced by the arguments presented and want to find out more or recommit to your faith, then good. But it can only come from you.

Why a survival guide?

A survival guide is what the Church needs at the moment. It's not that Catholicism cannot defend itself, but in recent years so many competing ideas and lifestyles have made it more difficult for young Catholics, in particular, to engage rationally with their faith.

But when challenged, shouldn't we turn the other cheek...?

From reading scripture, we know that Jesus was not a person who agreed with everyone. Neither was he someone who avoided conflict. On the contrary, Jesus was one of the most controversial figures in history. He was constantly arguing with and challenging the people who were in authority – he even told off his followers. Apart from the time he cleansed the Temple, Jesus was never physically violent and he never resorted to force, or the threat of it, but his style of debate could be considered confrontational at times.

We should be like that: non-violent, but always willing to make our point and argue for our faith. We should also remember that not only do we have the right to defend our faith and to tell the truth about it – we have a duty to do so.

Symbols and their meaning:

Here we explain the meaning of some important Catholic terms.

The "Did you know?" facts take topics from the chapter and explore them in more depth.

The "Think, pray or do" sections give you the opportunity to ponder, pray and act on your own, or to share each task with others. Either way, each action will be enriching.

I believe...

The Catholic Church contains the pure truth about human life – everything that you need to live a fulfilling, happy and productive life: from embryo to death, and beyond. It is honest, miraculous and wonderful. It is also entirely logical and reasonable.

Jesus Christ is real and the Catholic Church is Jesus' wish for every human being who has ever or will ever live. I cannot force you to believe anything (nor can anyone else). But my challenge to you may be simply expressed – be brave! Think deeply and honestly about the Catholic faith. Try not to be proud. If it speaks to you, follow it.

We are, because God is

"Nature gave man
two ends – one to
sit on and one to
think with. Ever
since then man's
success or failure
has been dependent
on the one he used
most."

George R. Kirkpatrick

We are, because God is

If you are like most people, you have probably asked one of the following questions at some point: "Who am I?" or "What is the purpose of my life?" Throughout history there have been a huge number of proposed answers.

The Christian faith starts from the simple premise that God created everything, including us – and the origin of our existence is a key subject of the Bible. So if you want to know who you are and your life's purpose, start by looking at the creator's revelation in the scriptures. For Catholics, an important starting point is the book of Genesis. This book explores the origins of the world and the human race – what we were, what we are now, and what we hope to be.

In this chapter we take a journey from creation all the way to Christ. We review how the Bible was formed, and we answer some of the most common criticisms of the "Good Book".

From creation to Christ – in less than one thousand words

God created everything to be perfect: the animals, the birds, the fish, the vegetation, and all that lives on the earth. But even though God pronounced these creations "good", none of them bore God's likeness. So God created a special being made in God's image, with an intellect and a will so that he or she might know, praise and love the creator.

Having free will meant that the first human beings could choose what to do: either stay close to God, which is what God wanted, or go away from God. God may have done this for a number of reasons. Perhaps because having a friend or companion who cannot independently choose to be with you, is not really having a friend or companion at all.

On account of their **sin**, however, the first humans distanced themselves from God, losing

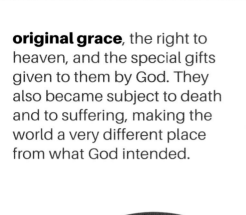

Sin

It describes two separate realities: original sin and actual sin. Original sin is the sin by which the first humans disobeyed God, thereby losing their original holiness and becoming subject to death. Actual (or personal) sin is any deliberate offence in thought, word, or deed, against the will of God.

original grace, the right to heaven, and the special gifts given to them by God. They also became subject to death and to suffering, making the world a very different place from what God intended.

Original grace

God's free gift to us, which helps us to live in keeping with God's call.

Martyr

A person who voluntarily suffers death for the sake of his or her faith, or in defence of a virtue.

But God did not forget us, because it was always God's plan that we should, in our own time, be with God for ever. So God sent God's prophets to guide us back. Throughout human history, very special men and women have served God by bringing God's message to the world, helping people to find God in their lives. Because what they tell us is something that we don't always want to hear, many have been killed. These people are called **martyrs** and they are very special to the Church because they put God above their own lives. Note, however, that while they are prepared to die for their faith, they would never kill for it.

Then God did something so strange, so extraordinary and original: God sent his only son, Jesus Christ, to restore the shattered relationship between human beings and God. Jesus was divine, still with the same infinite power that he always had. But he was also wholly human: he joined with us in all of the pain, desire, suffering and disappointment that we all feel at some time in our lives.

God (the Father) and Jesus (the Son) were inseparable in their mission, willing and yearning to take on the utmost – even the death of Jesus through crucifixion – out of love for humanity.

Following his crucifixion and through the will of his Father, Jesus was brought back to life in the resurrection. He overcame death and opened heaven's gates for everyone who would acknowledge and accept him. Now, through Jesus, we can proceed back to God. We don't need to be rich or clever, we just need to want it.

When Jesus returned to his Father in heaven the Holy Spirit was sent, equally divine, who shares the same mission as the Son and the Father. Jesus also established the Catholic Church. He did this through one of his apostles, Peter, whom he appointed to be the visible head of the Church. The purpose of the Church is to preserve and proclaim Jesus' teachings and to make present his sacrifice and sacraments for the salvation of everyone, until the end of time.

It is easy to forget, especially when facing difficulties in our lives, that Jesus is still with us. A failed exam, divorcing parents, the death of a loved one – at moments like these, Jesus is beside us, sharing our human suffering and bidding us to keep faith, to be patient and to trust in him. This makes our personal relationship with him special.

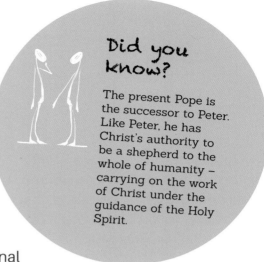

So here we are, over two thousand years later, living a life that is often difficult and confusing. But we do this with the companionship of Jesus Christ, God who comes to us not as a distant and authoritative ruler, but as a friend, protector and brother.

But how do we know all of this?

The Bible and its history

The Bible is a collection of seventy-two books, written at different times by many different individuals. It is divided into the Old Testament and the New Testament. The Old Testament is the original Jewish scripture, which was written in Hebrew between the years 900 and 160 BC. It records God's dealings with the Israelites, God's "chosen people", and their response to God's divine plan. The New Testament was written in Greek between the years AD 50 and 140. It focuses on the life and resurrection of Jesus, and the establishment of the Church.

In the Catholic Bible there are forty-six books included in the Old Testament, the same number used by the early Church. This version comes from a Greek translation of the scriptures known as the "Septuagint" and was used by many Jews at the time of Jesus. Where the Old Testament is referred to in the New Testament, the Septuagint text is almost always quoted.

During and after Jesus' time on earth, many Christians wrote about his life, the Church and the spread of Christianity. These writings include the Gospels of Matthew, Mark, Luke and John, the Acts of the Apostles, the Epistles (letters) of St Paul, other epistles, and the book of Revelation.

By the year AD 200 there were hundreds of texts in circulation. It actually took around three hundred years after the last book of the New Testament (The Revelation of St John) was penned for the Church to sift through the many and varied books, deciding which were authentic and could be believed.

The process demanded a lot of effort and attention, with great care taken to ensure only the books that could be relied on were included. Two simple questions were considered: "Can we trace the material in this

Gospel back to an eyewitness, or at least someone who knew an eyewitness?" and "Does this Gospel support the genuine teaching of the Church as it has always been understood?" In the end, it was decided that only four Gospels could be trusted, namely Matthew, Mark, Luke and John.

When Christianity became the official religion of the Roman Empire in the fourth century, it became possible for Christians to celebrate their faith openly without fear of persecution. During this period and for part of the fifth century, a number of councils were held and the Catholic Bible, which we still use today, was finalised. The Church remains the only reliable authority for its ongoing interpretation.

Is the "Good Book" bad?

Much of the criticism of Christianity focuses on the books of the Old Testament. So how can we respond to the accusation, which is often made, that the Old Testament is full of wars, violence, incest, murder, cruelty and general mayhem?

The violent events found in much of the Old Testament can best be understood by putting them into context: the Old Testament tells the story of a people – the Jewish people – falling in and out of grace with God. Their journey, like any other human journey, is at times painful. They suffered and caused a fair amount of suffering too.

The Christian explanation for the state of the world at this time is that humanity had become disastrously flawed; it had moved away from God to the extent that wrong deeds had become normal.

The Jews were waiting for something to change, anticipating a time that they would be set free from their hardships and their "captivity to sin". Catholics believe that this freedom, or salvation, was provided in the person of Jesus. God established God's final covenant with the human race – Jews and non-Jews – through Jesus Christ to restore our lost union with his Father.

So, yes, Catholics accept that there is a lot of violence and mayhem in the Old Testament, and at times God appears distant and harsh, judgemental and unforgiving, even cruel. Yet within all of that, we also see in the Bible God's love as God continues to care for God's chosen people, reach out to God's wider creation, and draw us all towards God.

"Because it says so in the Bible!"

Does the Bible really contain accurate details of history, or is it filled with lots of myths and legends that can only be interpreted properly by people who have faith?

There are certain things contained in the Bible that must be true if we are to call our faith reasonable and logical. They include:

- An historical Jesus
- Apostles
- A place called Galilee
- A man named Paul, and so on

These are a few of the "physical facts" of our faith. Fortunately, for the past two thousand years the evidence in favour of the physical facts recorded in the New Testament hold up very well to historical and archaeological enquiry. There is a lot of evidence supporting both the geographical, cultural and personal descriptions given in the New Testament, often more so than for some historical figures whose existence very few people question.

It should be noted, however, that we can't "prove" the Bible is authentic simply by referring to the Bible itself. So we can't say: "Well, Jesus was the Son of God because it says so in the Bible." We need to look at when, why and how the Bible was written and put together to establish if the things it contains can be considered accurate or not. It does help, though, to realise that of the Gospel writers both Matthew and John knew Jesus personally, and that Mark and Luke were very close to other followers of Jesus who knew him. This makes the idea that the events they agree on were "made up" unconvincing.

When the New Testament accounts and the letters of St Paul were written (during AD 50–80), there would have been thousands of people around who had seen Jesus, listened to him teach and witnessed the events of his life. Think about that! If you had seen something with your own eyes and then read an account of the same event in which something completely different was described, wouldn't you say something?

Do Catholics believe that the world was created in six days?

Catholics do not believe that everything contained in the Bible is a literal fact.

If we look at Genesis, for example, we read that God made everything in six days and then had a day off. Then God made a man out of dust. Shortly after that God made a woman out of the man's rib. God put them in a garden, which was paradise, but they misbehaved and so God had to throw them out. The couple had children, who had other children, and so on, and lots of good and bad things happened to them.

So what are we to make of this account? Well, if you took it at face value you could be forgiven for closing this book right now and getting on with your life. This biblical description clearly contradicts what we now know about the age and origins of the universe and the human race. When we talk about cosmology and evolution we measure things in billions or millions of years, not days. So the idea that two fully formed human beings (one made from a part of the other) lived in a garden around four thousand five hundred years ago, just after the world was made, and who went on to populate the earth, is too hard to accept as a literal fact.

It might be reassuring then to know that we don't have to. The Catholic Church has long considered part of the Bible, including the creation accounts of Genesis to be **allegory**, rather than historical description.

As Catholics we could, therefore, say that Genesis means something like:

God is the instigator and maker of all creation. Nothing could have existed without God. God has no precedent, meaning that God has always been there and will always be there. The universe God created provided an environment in which organic life, and eventually human beings, could come about. All of this was willed and nurtured by God. Whether it took billions of years or for organisms to come about through natural selection is not that important.

Notice that in no way have we sidestepped the awkward question of God's personal hand in the creation of humanity. There is nothing in theories such as the Big Bang or evolution that can prove or disprove this basic and essential fact of Christian faith. All that is important is that God created everything and that, at some point, human beings came into being as a distinct and unique species.

The creation accounts of Genesis highlight one of the difficulties of just picking up the Bible, especially the Old Testament, and reading it alone. This is because it's not always clear what some of the texts mean. They require interpretation – which the Church has the authority to do. That does not mean that you should be afraid to read the Bible on your own. It simply means that you can rely on the Church to explain anything that you find challenging.

Allegory

A story, poem or picture that can be interpreted to reveal a hidden meaning, typically a moral one.

Catholics are called to be "co-workers" with God in the work of creation. What does this mean to you? Identify three things that you can do to help make the world what God wants it to be.

I believe

"In God, the Father almighty... and in Jesus Christ, his only Son... I believe in the Holy Spirit."

I believe

The central mystery of our Christian faith is the Trinity. God is revealed to us as three divine persons of the Trinity: the Father, the Son and the Holy Spirit. Yet the Father, the Son and the Holy Spirit are not three Gods, but one God. Trying to understand how we hold this belief is baffling for many people – including Catholics.

In this chapter we look at the three persons of the Trinity, showing how they are united and how each is distinct, and how they relate to us. One way of trying to make sense of it is by looking at ourselves. Many of us have three names: a first name, a middle name and a last name. Standing alone, each of those three names represents who each of us is, but none of the three names alone represents our whole name; only all three names together can do that. That is somewhat like the Holy Trinity.

Who made God?

Questions like, "Who made God?" and "Where did God come from?" set obvious limits on God's nature – limits that Catholics should reject because in the context of God, there are no limits. In answer to questions like these, we would say that God is the "necessary being". This means that he had no creator; he has always been there. This is a belief arrived at through faith and reason.

God the Father

The first person of the Trinity is God the Father. Many Catholics perceive the Father as a remote figure. The "white-bearded God" sitting on a cloud is the way artists in the west have represented God for centuries. There is nothing wrong with this. It would be a problem, though, if we thought of God only as a very smart version of a human being, because this would place limits on who and what God is. There are no limits to God whatsoever.

When we profess in the Nicene Creed that the Father is "maker of heaven and earth, of all things visible and invisible", we are saying that we acknowledge that God is the source of all life and that all of creation exists because God willed it. God loves all of creation, especially humanity. We know that because God the Father sent his only Son, Jesus Christ, to restore the bond between human beings and God.

In the Gospels Jesus calls his Father *Abba*. This suggests that, like God's relationship with humanity, there is a loving bond between the Father and his Son. And it is his Son, Jesus, who is the second person of the Trinity.

Is God male?

God is a pure spirit so God has no physical body. This means he can be neither male nor female. Only the second person of the Trinity, Jesus, took on a human nature and had an actual human body, which was male.

While Christianity believes that God is Father, Son and Holy Spirit, the use of the masculine pronoun "he" is often used to refer to God. When it is used in this way it is not meant to suggest that God is male, or has any gender.

God the Son

The difficulty of imagining God the Father might explain why many of us find it easier to picture his Son, Jesus. Jesus is God, completely and absolutely – he is the incarnation of God (incarnation simply means "made flesh"). So Jesus is God made flesh. He is also entirely human. There are several passages in the scriptures to support our understanding of Jesus' two natures – divine and human. For example:

- The prologue of John's Gospel says: "The Word was made flesh, he lived among us, and we saw his glory, the glory that is his as the only Son of the Father, full of grace and truth" (John 1:14).

- Mark's Gospel specifically refers to Jesus as the "Son of God". He does this several times – at Jesus' baptism, when he casts out the unclean spirits, during the transfiguration and when a Roman centurion acknowledges Jesus at the cross.

- Matthew's Gospel informs us, perhaps most tellingly, that Jesus asks his disciples who they think he is and Peter rightly calls him "the Christ, the Son of the Living God" (Matthew 16:16).

Throughout the four Gospels we hear that Jesus healed the sick, raised the dead and performed miracles in which the physical laws of the universe appeared to be suspended: he walked on water, calmed a violent storm and, after his execution, conquered death itself. This is impressive, to say the least, and each of these remarkable deeds confirms what we believe to be true about Jesus: that he is one with God the Father.

One of the most common questions asked about Jesus is: why did he have to come to earth as a human being and die a horrific death in order to save us? The peculiar problem of being human is at the heart of God's solution to sin. Every human being, man, woman and child, has free will. This means that we are able to make choices. The problem that creates is this: if we are separated from God through original sin and/or our own sins, then how can we, through our own actions, be restored to God? If God created us to have free will, how can God restore us to grace without doing it for us, and thereby overriding our free will?

Jesus is the bridge who makes this reconciliation possible. He enters into human experience by becoming totally human. He is tempted, suffers greatly, is persecuted and dies. He is the voluntary and complete sacrifice, literally killed by his own creation – despite being entirely blameless.

In this way, by totally participating in our humanity, he is able to assume upon himself the burden of original sin, to restore us to God's favour. Our independence of will is still intact. This means that we are still responsible for our own conduct. But thankfully, through Jesus' sacrifice, we are no longer – unless we choose – separated from God.

It is an ingenious solution to what seems to be an unsolvable problem. It is also the perfect demonstration of God's love and desire that we are reconciled to God. On top of our salvation, Jesus also leaves us with the most perfect example of what it means to be fully human and a beautiful set of values to live by.

The Holy Spirit

The third person of the Trinity is the Holy Spirit, who is often a source of confusion for Catholics. This is largely because we find the Holy Spirit hard to visualise. It is a common mistake to consider the Holy Spirit as a "power" or "force" coming from God (like in that well-known science fiction film). This is wrong, because the Holy Spirit is both a person and God in his own right, exactly like Jesus and the Father – God the Father, God the Son and God the Holy Spirit.

The Holy Spirit is and always has been active in the world. It was the Holy Spirit who gave the universe life, led Jesus into the desert and who comes to us through baptism and offers us his gifts in confirmation. From the Holy Spirit we receive gifts such as wisdom, understanding and knowledge. Other gifts include faith, healing, miracles, love, joy, peace, patience, kindness, goodness, faithfulness, gentleness and self-control. He also gives life to the Church, inspiring its ongoing mission. But, perhaps, the Holy Spirit is best known for bringing Jesus into being in Mary's womb.

So what more do we know about Mary?

There's something about Mary

It is entirely fair to say that the Virgin Mary was unlike any other human being who has ever lived. She was born without original sin, which means that she was in no way separated from God. While she may not have known the full extent of what God wanted from her, she accepted God's will. In fact Mary is the perfect example of what it means to be in an open and face-to-face relationship with God. This is a vital point in understanding who Mary was and what she was able to become.

Consider the situation Mary found herself in: at a young age she is confronted by an angel who tells her that she has been chosen to bear God's own Son, who will be the saviour of humanity. How would you respond to this news? Despite Mary's feelings – which were likely to be those of awe and wonder – she was able to respond rationally. She made a choice to exercise fully the free will that God has given her and she says: "Let what you have said be done to me."

As Jesus grows in age, Mary watches over her son as he embarks on his mission of salvation. When that mission reaches its completion, she bravely stays by Jesus' side as he is put to death in the most violent way on the cross. Jesus repays her love infinitely. In his final moments, he entrusts his mother's safety to the apostle John (and also his to her).

So we see that the divine plan reaches a definitive moment when Mary accepts the Father's will to bear his Son. Because of that we can say with no anxiety that Mary is truly the Mother of God.

She did something astounding. And what we should not forget is that Mary was a teenage girl when she accepted God's will at a time and place when teenage girls were often seen, but unheard.

If we are only supposed to worship God, why do we pray to Mary?

There is a distinction to be drawn between worship and devotion. Only God – the Father, Son and Holy Spirit – is worthy of worship, but devotion can take many forms. We may be devoted to a saint, to the Virgin Mary, to the Rosary, to icons and so on. What this means is that we recognise God's grace as present within them, not that they are objects of worship in themselves. So it is fine, for example, to pray to the Virgin Mary or to any saint to ask for their prayers to God on our behalf.

What is the Immaculate Conception?

In Catholicism we talk of the Immaculate Conception, which people sometimes mistakenly believe is the conception of Jesus. It fact it refers to the conception of Mary herself, when her mother Anne became pregnant. Mary was born without original sin – therefore there was nothing preventing her from understanding (to what extent is unknown) what God wanted of her. Because of this she was able to give her full consent to what was being asked of her. It was her decision to say yes.

When you hear the phrase "Jesus saves", what does it mean to you? How would you describe what it means to a non-Christian?"

Being Catholic

"Even the turtle
would get nowhere
if he didn't stick out
his neck."

Croft M. Pentz

Being Catholic

Ever been asked why you are a Catholic, or wondered why those around you do not share your faith? This chapter explores what Catholics mean by faith and shows up some of the common myths about being a Catholic.

What is faith?

Our faith is like falling in love. It is a grand romantic gesture – perhaps the grandest. And, like falling in love, it is not necessarily something that you have control over. It just happens. To be more specific, faith is a virtue that is God-given and every person is free to accept or reject it.

Faith is a high-wire act – risky and courageous – because you don't know what you are getting into. Because of this, it is exciting – even daring.

We have faith in God, in Jesus and in the teaching of our Church, but we do not know these are true in the same way that we know if a tree or a chair or a dog exists or not. That's why we have expressions like "leap of faith", meaning to trust in something beyond our ordinary senses.

Faith is also a deeply creative act from which new things arise – like writing a book or a poem, or drawing a picture or composing song lyrics. We do not know where the words or images come from in the same way that we know we are holding a pen or a pencil, or a musical instrument.

There is no experiment that proves faith, any more than there is an experiment that proves love or creativity – they remain the mystery at the very heart of our humanity. Faith is a mystery – but real nonetheless.

The Catholic feeling

A confirmation group was once asked what it felt like to be Catholic. Amid the more expected answers, a girl said that her faith was like floating in the open sea. She went on to explain that her family were keen sailors and, whenever possible, they would set off along the south coast in their yacht, finding a quiet cove or bay where they could go swimming.

She liked to swim some way from the boat and to float on her back, looking up at the sky, drifting on the tide. It was while doing this that she experienced what is sometimes described as an "oceanic feeling". Oddly enough, an oceanic feeling doesn't really have anything to do with oceans, but is a sensation of being deeply connected to everything in a way that feels almost supernatural:

physical boundaries are blurred, distance and time lose their meaning, and the person feels as if they are at the centre of everything. It is often used to describe a religious experience, when a person somehow "feels" the presence of God around him or her and through him or her.

Floating in the sea, aware of the huge weight of water below and around her, she felt an intense sensation of being connected to everything, everywhere. This feeling lasted for about a minute, but it gave her a remarkable idea of how everything could be brought together, unified in a single experience, which she related to her faith.

There was once a story that went as follows...

A defendant was on trial for murder. There was strong evidence indicating guilt, but there was no corpse. In the defence's closing statement, the lawyer, knowing that his client would probably be convicted, resorted to a trick.

"Ladies and gentlemen of the jury, I have a surprise for you," he said.

"Within one minute, the person presumed dead in this case will walk into this courtroom."

The jurors, somewhat stunned, all looked on eagerly at the courtroom door. A minute passed but nothing happened. Finally, the lawyer said: "Actually, I made up the previous statement. But you looked with anticipation. I, therefore, put it to you that there is reasonable doubt in this case as to whether anyone was killed and insist that you return a verdict of not guilty."

The jury retired to deliberate. A few minutes later, they returned and pronounced a verdict of guilty.

"But how?" enquired the lawyer. "You must have had some doubt. I saw all of you stare at the door." The jury foreman replied: "Yes, we did look. But your client did not."

True or false?

The Catholic faith has long been the target of suspicion and hostility. But how much of this is based on ignorance and prejudice, and how much of it is the fruit of thoughtful consideration of the facts? By separating fact from fiction, we can see that much popular opinion about Catholicism is based on misunderstanding and misinformation – and in fact that the Catholic faith is rich and true.

Myth one: obsessed with sin

One of the most common accusations made against Catholics is that we are obsessed with sin. Picture the scene: a little, old lady dripping with guilt, dreading the wrath of God, counts her Rosary

Did you know?

The Catholic Church is among the oldest of the world's institutions and has been more influential in the history of Western civilisation, if not the whole world, than any other. Around the globe it provides more school places, medicine and aid than any other non-governmental organisation.

beads as a form of punishment for being "bad".

Sound like anyone you know? Not likely. But it is easy to see how this idea may have taken hold, if only among people who don't really know a lot about being Catholic. It's true that Catholics are encouraged to participate in the sacrament of reconciliation (often referred to as "confession"), in which we are invited to confess those things that we have got wrong and to ask for forgiveness. Often we begin Mass with the public confession, "I confess to almighty God..." This is something that some non-Catholics probably find quite strange. So is this evidence that Catholics are obsessed with sin? Some people might say so, but they would be wrong. Catholics are not obsessed with sin and guilt – our obsession is with forgiveness and the remarkable kindness of a God who wants nothing more than for us to choose to be forgiven by God when we get things wrong.

God's readiness to forgive is the only possible answer to sin. God's forgiveness, and our own, helps us to live healthily – free from anxiety and free from guilt.

Myth two: rigid followers of rules

It is a remarkable truth that our universe depends entirely on very precise physical laws. Should these vary, even slightly, then everything that we know would simply not exist.

When we hear people say things like "The universe is entirely random, there is no order to anything" or "Everything only happens by chance" we might wonder which universe it is they are talking about, because it doesn't really sound like ours.

We should therefore not be too surprised that the God who made our orderly universe also established laws for us to live by – laws that we should place at the very centre of our lives.

People sometimes say that Catholics are too rigid in the way that we follow God's laws and that our "rules" somehow prevent us from being truly "free". But this is to mistake God's purpose in establishing such laws and to misunderstand how we actually feel about them. God's laws are not there to entrap us or to make us obsessive rule followers. They are the means by which we can understand God's revelation with confidence, knowing God's authentic voice.

God's laws set us truly free because they show us how to live in a loving and faithful relationship with God, which gives our lives meaning and fulfilment. Love, kindness and compassion, family, relationships, community, peace, sharing, hope and joy – these are some of the gifts that flow abundantly from God's laws. And just as knowledge of the physical laws of the universe prevents us from assuming that everything is chaotic and disordered, so too does knowledge of God's laws prevent us from believing that our lives are without purpose or importance.

The laws also work both ways – just as God wants us to keep our promises to God, we want God to keep God's promises to us.

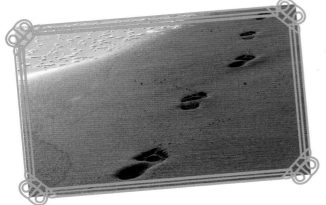

God has placed God in an agreement with every human being and has promised that if we honestly try to live according to God's laws then all of God's promises will be fulfilled in return. And God doesn't expect us to be perfect. In fact God expects us to get things wrong and is willing to forgive us anything if we only ask for forgiveness.

There are many expressions of God's laws (for example, natural law, the Law of the Old Testament, the law of the Gospel and Church law), but they are perfected and completed in Jesus himself, in whom all law is fulfilled: "For Christ is the end of the Law, that everyone who has faith may be justified" (Romans 10:4).

And how should we live in order to fulfil God's law? By following the two simple commandments that Jesus asked of us: love God and love one another.

To follow Jesus is not to live in servitude, slavery or fear. It is not the denial of choice, but the affirmation of the greatest freedom that can be imagined. We gain the freedom to be exactly what we were created to be – to be ourselves – joyful and hopeful people, in a personal and loving relationship with God.

Myth three: idolatry of the Pope

While warning against the dangers of worshipping celebrities, sporting personalities and reality TV stars, does Catholics' excessive love or worship of a little man in a white cassock make us guilty of idolatry – the worship of a false god?

The answer is: Catholics worship God and only God. This is because only God is worthy of worship. While we depend on the Pope and look to him for counsel and guidance, we do not, in any way, worship him or give him the praise due to God alone.

The Pope is the head of the Catholic Church, the successor to St Peter, who was chosen by Jesus to lead the Church after Our Lord's ascension. The words Jesus used are among the most famous and the clearest in the whole Bible:

> *"But you," he said "who do you say I am?" Then Simon Peter spoke up, "You are the Christ," he said, "the Son of the living God." Jesus replied, "Simon son of Jonah, you are a happy man! Because it was not flesh and blood that revealed this to you but my Father in heaven. So I now say to you: You are Peter and on this rock I will build my Church. And the gates of the underworld can never hold out against it. I will give you the keys of the kingdom of heaven: whatever you bind on earth shall be considered bound in heaven; whatever you loose on earth shall be considered loosed in heaven."*
>
> *Matthew 16:16-19*

The word "Peter" actually means "rock". Used by Jesus it highlights Peter's position as the rock on which God's Church shall be built. Peter, therefore, and all future popes, have authority over the Church on earth.

These powerful and moving words of Our Lord give some idea as to why Catholics show great respect to the Pope: why we are so joyful to see him and be in his presence, why people will wait for hours, sometimes days, to be near him or hear him offer Mass, and why millions every year go to St Peter's Square in Rome hoping for a glimpse of him.

We feel like this because we know that the Pope is the Holy Spirit's chosen successor to St Peter, tasked with caring for us before Jesus returns. We also know that the Pope stands in a unique relationship with the Holy Spirit – as he is able, through divine inspiration, to guide the Church soundly and to determine infallibly matters of faith and morality. This means that we can rely on him to guide us faithfully and honestly towards God.

What does being a Catholic mean to you? If you were asked by someone, "Why are you a Catholic?", how would you respond?

Introduction to the Mass and the sacraments

St Teresa was overwhelmed with God's goodness and asked Our Lord, "How can I thank you?" Our Lord replied, "ATTEND ONE MASS."

Introduction to the Mass and the sacraments

Perhaps a common cause of conflict between parents and their children concerns Sunday Mass. Many parents are probably familiar with the following words: "I'm not going to Church because it's boring" or "I don't have to go to Church to believe in God". If you find attending Church boring or unnecessary, you are not the first. But a careful read of this chapter on the Mass could make you change your mind and give you a new appreciation of why participating in the Mass is so important in God's plan for you.

What is Mass?

At the centre of Catholicism is the Mass, the church service over which a priest must preside. It has at its heart the consecration – the moment when the bread and wine are "**transubstantiated**" into the body and blood of Jesus. When we celebrate the Eucharist together, we are in communion with every other Catholic who has ever lived and who will ever live. It is the ultimate communal event.

Transubstantiation

The change that takes place when the bread and wine become the body and blood of Jesus Christ during Mass. Only the appearances (taste, smell and the like) of bread and wine remain.

To the Catholic Church the Mass is the "source and summit of the Christian life". Everything else, including the other sacraments, is directed towards it.

The Mass usually lasts between forty minutes and an hour, depending on the size of the congregation and the season of the Church's year. Not every Mass is the same. The readings change, so do the vestments (robes) the **celebrant** wears. Again, this all depends on the season, as well as the day of the week the Mass is on and whether or not it is a "special day". While the details of the Mass may change, the Mass is always made up of the following four parts:

1. **Introductory rites**
2. **Liturgy of the Word**
3. **Liturgy of the Eucharist**
4. **Concluding rites**

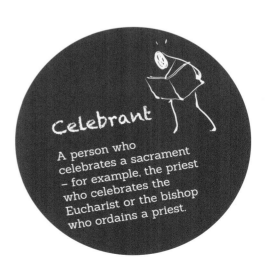

Celebrant

A person who celebrates a sacrament – for example, the priest who celebrates the Eucharist or the bishop who ordains a priest.

Educating the "masses"

Introductory Rites

The priest enters, sometimes with a deacon and altar servers. He usually invites the congregation to take part in the Penitential Act. This is a public acknowledgement that we are not perfect, we get things wrong and we are all in need of God's forgiveness. This is usually followed by the Gloria, which praises God.

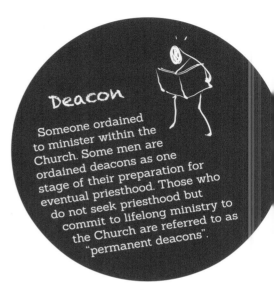

Deacon

Someone ordained to minister within the Church. Some men are ordained deacons as one stage of their preparation for eventual priesthood. Those who do not seek priesthood but commit to lifelong ministry to the Church are referred to as "permanent deacons".

Liturgy of the Word

Three scripture readings are usually given:

- **The first is from the Old Testament (or the Acts of the Apostles during Easter), followed by a psalm**
- **The second is from the New Testament, typically – but not exclusively – from one of St Paul's letters**
- **The third is from a Gospel. This can only be read by a priest or a deacon**

Next, a homily is given, usually related to the readings or the liturgy of the day, and finally the **Creed** is spoken aloud by the congregation.

Creed

A summary of Christian beliefs. The most familiar creeds are the Apostles' Creed and the Nicene Creed.

Liturgy of the Eucharist

This part of the Mass focuses on the consecration of the bread and wine into the body and blood of Christ. It begins with the priest placing the gifts of bread and wine on the altar. He follows this by saying the exact words spoken by Jesus at the Last Supper: "This is my body" (over the bread) and "This is the chalice of my blood" (over the wine). The changing of the bread and wine into the body and blood of Jesus Christ means that Jesus is truly, though mysteriously, present in these gifts. The gifts of Christ's body and blood are offered up in sacrifice, connecting each Mass to Christ's death on the cross. Once this part of the Mass is complete, the Lord's Prayer ("Our Father") is prayed and Holy Communion is given to those who are in full communion with the Catholic Church.

Concluding Rites

A prayer and blessing end the Mass and the congregation is dismissed. Sometimes a few brief announcements precede the blessing at this time. The priest will then say "Go in peace" or something similar, and we respond, "Thanks be to God".

And that's when our work really begins...

Before Mass

Take a few minutes before Mass to get yourself in the right mood. You are, after all, going to have a close encounter with Jesus in the Eucharist, so you should be in a prayerful and reflective state of mind.

You are not supposed to eat or drink anything during the hour before Holy Communion. This rule does not apply to anyone who is old, ill or taking medicine.

During Mass

A priest once said that the Mass was not there to entertain you, but to provide you with graces and spiritual fulfilment. This is undoubtedly true, but people are people and sometimes concentration can wane, which is a polite way of saying that they get bored. If you don't understand what is going on, Mass can seem like an hour of the same old thing, week after week. However, try to think about what you have learnt about the parts of the Mass, including the meaning of the scripture readings. The more you learn, the more you will appreciate the miracle that takes place at every Mass. Until you get to that point, at least enjoy the quiet time and meditation.

After Mass

It is good to make a prayer of thanksgiving before leaving church and to maintain an atmosphere of prayer for other people to keep praying.

Before you leave, you could quietly say something like:

> Lord Jesus, thank you for the sacrifice you made for me, my family and the entire world. Help each of us to appreciate more fully what it means to eat and drink your body and blood, and continue to nourish us with your knowledge and love, as you did for your first disciples. Amen.

The Eucharist

Does the bread and wine really turn into Jesus Christ?

When the priest says the words of consecration, there is a real change in the bread and wine. Nothing is left of the bread and wine but the appearance alone. Beneath the appearance Christ is truly present.

We accept and honour his "real presence" by prayerful adoration because this is the personal presence of the Son of God, who invites us to respond in a relationship of faith, hope and love.

Can non-Catholics receive communion?

Communion means being in union with God and with one another in belief. This means only those who share the Catholic faith can be invited to communion.

Does the Penitential Act at the beginning of Mass replace the need to go to confession?

No.

The sacraments

The Latin word *sacramentum* means a "pledge" or "promise" or "token". The sacraments of the Catholic Church are pledges, promises or tokens she calls "visible signs of grace", given by Jesus and entrusted to his Church. There are seven sacraments. Each contains particular graces, bringing us closer to God:

Baptism

Baptism is the first step in a lifelong journey of commitment and discipleship. Whether we are baptised as an infant or an adult, baptism unites us to Christ and to the Church, as each baptised person is "marked with the indelible seal of Christ".

Eucharist

Catholics believe the Eucharist, or communion, is both a sacrifice and a meal. We believe in the Real Presence of Jesus, who died for our sins. As we receive Christ's body and blood, we are nourished spiritually and brought closer to God.

Reconciliation

The Catholic sacrament of reconciliation has four elements: contrition, confession and satisfaction (penance) and absolution. In it we find God's unconditional forgiveness. As a result, we are called to forgive others.

Confirmation

Confirmation completes the grace of baptism by confirming (or "sealing") the baptised person's union with Christ and by equipping that person for active participation in the life of the Church.

Marriage

The sacrament of marriage, or holy matrimony, is a public sign that two people give themselves to each other unconditionally. It is also a public statement about God: the loving union of a husband and wife is an affirmation of openness to new life, and the unbreakable relationship of Christ to his Church.

Holy Orders

In the sacrament of holy orders, or ordination, the priest, deacon or bishop being ordained vows to lead other Catholics – by bringing them the sacraments, by proclaiming the Gospel, and by providing other means to holiness.

Anointing of the Sick

The anointing of the sick is a ritual of healing – appropriate not only for physical, but also for mental and spiritual sickness.

The Church advises us to prepare spiritually before receiving Holy Communion so that we can receive the body and blood of Jesus with faith and devotion. Identify *three* things that you can do to prepare to receive the sacrament of the Eucharist.

Morality and justice – part 1

"You've only got three choices in life: give up, give in, or give it all you've got."

Unknown

Few topics lead to awkward conversations and uneasiness quite like sex. Some Catholics still associate sex with the word "No!" But this is a mistake. Sex should be a beautiful and truly enjoyable experience, which has the power to deepen and cement the relationship between two people within a permanent relationship. It is unfortunate that this view of sex is not often identified as "Catholic".

This chapter takes an honest look at sex and explores the tough questions and challenges of Church teaching on it. It also looks at the issues of relationships, marriage, virginity, celibacy, and what to do if you lose yourself to temptation.

Sex and relationships: let's talk about "it"

At no time in history have so many expectations been piled on young adults starting out in life. The pressure to succeed at school, at university, and to be popular and attractive can seem relentless. For some the effect is damaging, with expectations so high that depression, low self-esteem and general misery often result.

Decisions about sexual conduct during this time can be particularly hard to make and the Church recognises that it can be especially difficult for young Catholics who also have to take on board the Church's teaching on sex and relationships, which has often been presented as rigid and out of sync with popular opinion.

Fortunately the Church is getting better at explaining the joys of sex, acknowledging the sexual union between a man and a woman as having a much deeper meaning than a purely biological one – as it was once considered. This change in attitude is helping to give a more positive view of human sexuality.

Of its nature, sex is a physical act, but its "deeper meaning" refers to the fact that sex has the power to heal, to comfort and to reassure. Through their sexual union a couple come to a deeper understanding of each other, and this promotes growth, trust and security. Sex can also help couples to express their love and commitment to each other, and to communicate the deepest thoughts, feelings and the needs of the partners. That's one of the reasons why the Catholic Church says that sex can only find full and authentic expression within the permanent commitment of marriage.

Sex outside of marriage is likely to be less fulfilling. First, because the two people involved can't be sure they mean the same thing: one partner, for example, might feel that the next step in the relationship is marriage, while the other person might be thinking more short-term. And second, because outside of marriage, sex doesn't have the chance to express its full potential. Making love should mean making love, and by couples giving themselves to each other sexually they can increase their love for each other and encourage it to grow.

What if I've already had sex?

If you've already had sex and regret that decision, the first step is to stop having sex and begin with a renewed commitment to not have sex. Your past does not have to determine your future. You can begin today. Second, ask yourself some tough questions: Why did I start having sex? Was I pressured into it? Was I looking for love and thought sex would fill that void? Did I think that everyone my age was "doing it"?

The last question is probably the easiest to answer. The proof is in human experience: for every person who may say or think, "I wish we had", there are probably many more that say or think, "I wish we hadn't".

Third and most important, be confident of God's forgiveness, which is always offered through the sacrament of reconciliation, just as we must confidently pray that God will forgive others for their mistakes.

Marriage: when two become one

While we have seen that the Church places great importance on marriage, fewer people than ever before are choosing to "get wed" – with many couples opting to cohabit instead. So, is marriage still relevant?

It should be obvious by now that the Catholic concept of marriage involves more than simply the wedding within the church, although, like everyone else, Catholics love a good wedding. However, what makes a marriage Christian is not a good knees-up following the ceremony, but a personal relationship of life-giving love in which two people make the love of Christ present to each other, and one in which the partners become a sign of love of Christ to those around them. This is a high ideal, a sacred ideal. And it's because of this that the Church supports and actively promotes marriage. In addition, marriage provides many benefits, one of which is stability. This is important because a stable family provides the best environment in which to bring up children, giving them the firm grounding and confidence they need to learn and grow. It is also the best environment for the husband and wife to grow together, and for their love to deepen as the years pass.

Why do Catholics have to get married in church?

When Catholics marry they believe that God ratifies their union. This is expressed during the wedding ceremony, in the words: "What God has joined together, let no man put asunder." Catholics see marriage as something that God is involved in: that is why the wedding takes place in church.

Virginity and celibacy: singled out

Like the "old, married couple", there are lots of stereotypes about grown-up virgins, and modern depictions like the 2005 film, *The 40-Year-Old Virgin* – about a man whose co-workers conspire to "hook him up" after they discover he has never done the deed. Surprisingly (or perhaps not), however, like marriage, maintaining the state of being a virgin is a challenge worthy of respect – not ridicule. The mother of Jesus remained a virgin. She was made pregnant by the Holy Spirit, not through sexual intercourse. Many saints and holy people were also described as virgins, and throughout the history of the Church virginity has been a highly prized virtue.

There are three obvious stages of Catholic virginity:

- **Childhood**
- **Adulthood – before marriage**
- **Adulthood – as part of a vocation**

It is perhaps from the first of these that we get our idea of the purity of virginity, because we instinctively recognise the innocence of children.

In adulthood, the Christian ideal is that virginity should be maintained until marriage.

People associated with the third group include those who have chosen a religious vocation that requires a lifelong commitment to remaining single (celibacy). A person may not always be a virgin before deciding to be celibate. For example, someone may undertake a religious vocation following the death of his or her spouse.

With such emphasis on virginity, can we conclude that the Catholic Church opposes sex? Of course not! Neither is virginity a "commodity"

– a thing to be held up like a trophy. It is important in relation to the good that it does. For instance, for those called to religious life, celibacy allows them to dedicate themselves to God and to their ministry in a very special way. Therefore, something good has resulted from their commitment.

Justice for all

Our faith is lived out in every part of our lives, not just once a week when we go to Mass. We are called to serve others and, in doing so, serve God, who is the source of all goodness and truth. Social justice is a term used to describe how we can achieve this essential goal – to serve others. It is important to remember that social justice is not a political movement or ideology, but rather a way in which we can live our lives as Catholics, caring for others and trying to ensure that no one is excluded from society.

This is why we campaign for an end to poverty, for education and healthcare for all, for true equality and inclusion, for no one to be persecuted or deprived of those things that God tells us are the right of everyone. It is how we live out the words of Jesus when he said: "As you did this to one of the least of these brothers of mine, you did it to me." (Matthew 25:40)

Dear Jesus, help me to see myself as you see me, and give me the strength and courage to accept myself and the values which I have learned from you. May a deep love of, respect for and service to others be the source of any pleasure that I seek or that is put before me. I would prefer not to be tested at all because I know how easy it can be to give in to temptation. I ask only that your grace be open to me so that I can be strengthened through your love. Amen.

Morality and justice – part 2

"Life is like a game of cards. The hand that is dealt you represents determinism; the way you play it is free will."

Jawaharlal Nehru

Abortion: countering with love

If we were to sum up the Church's teaching on abortion in a simple sentence we might say: "The unborn child is a human being and has a right to life." The Church takes this position because it believes that all human beings are sacred and must therefore be protected and loved.

God's commandment to "love our neighbour" extends to the unborn child, as much as it applies to a newborn baby, an infant, a teenager, an adult or an elderly person. The right to life does not change depending on the age of a person.

But as we strive to love all others, we must – if we are to adopt the truly Catholic position of being pro-life – extend our love to those who have chosen not to continue with their pregnancy. No matter how difficult, we have to resist the idea that someone who is thinking about having an abortion, or who has gone through with an abortion, is immoral, unworthy of compassion or not as good as us.

Their one mistake does not define them, just as our mistakes do not define us.

Any dialogue about abortion has to be motivated by compassion as well as a concern for standing up for what is right. Very often it is fear, panic and insecurity (or a lack of support or seeming lack of other options) that lead to an abortion, and those feelings can only be countered with love, compassion and understanding. In his first year as the leader of the Catholic Church, Pope Francis was instrumental in promoting a compassionate but uncompromising pro-life position.

Real life: Anna Romero

In 2013 an Italian divorcee, Anna Romero, discovered she was pregnant by a married man. The man tried to persuade her to have an abortion, but Anna made the difficult choice to go it alone and keep her baby. When she was still pregnant, she poured out her heart in a letter to Pope Francis. She addressed the envelope "Pope Francis, the Vatican" and posted it, never for one moment expecting a reply.

Imagine Anna's astonishment, then, when she answered the phone a short while later and immediately recognised the voice on the other end of the line as that of Pope Francis himself. Talking to her as a "dear friend", he reassured Anna that she would never be alone, and reminded her that a child is a gift from God and a sign of divine providence. He commended her for being "brave and strong" for her unborn child.

When Anna shared her fears about baptising her baby because she was divorced and a single mother, the Holy Father assured her that he would be her spiritual father, and even offered to baptise her baby himself.

Assisted suicide and euthanasia: the right to live

Like abortion, assisted suicide and euthanasia challenge the Church's pro-life stance. However, unlike abortion, they are currently illegal in English law. What this means is that it is illegal to help someone to kill themselves or to kill someone yourself. It doesn't matter if the person who dies asks you to help them to die, or asks you to kill them – they cannot give you "permission" to kill.

The Church agrees that this is right because it goes to the heart of what she believes: that all human life is sacred and cannot be replaced. As Jesus commanded, we all have a neighbourly duty to look after each other. This means preserving and protecting each other's lives.

Assisted suicide

The act of deliberately assisting or encouraging another person to kill themselves.

In those instances when people feel that their own lives are so intolerable or worthless that they would be better off dead, some have demanded the "right to die". There have been well-reported cases of people going to court to try to change the law to decriminalise voluntary **euthanasia** and **assisted suicide**. Some people have even gone to die abroad in countries where assisted suicide is legal.

Very often people who want to die are severely disabled or have crippling diseases like Parkinson's or multiple sclerosis, which have a serious effect on how they live. Sometimes they are very elderly and feel that they are a burden to those around them, so would be better off dead.

Euthanasia

The act of deliberately ending a person's life to relieve their suffering, either with or without their consent.

It is impossible not to feel great sympathy and love for people in these situations. But the answer is not death, but "love my neighbour". As a society we have a responsibility to properly care for everyone so that no one feels that their life is worthless. This may be intense and very painful at times, but it also provides opportunities for expressing love and gratitude, for spiritual growth and for reconciliation with God and one another.

Homosexuality: who am I to judge?

The Catholic Church's attitude towards homosexuality is considered by and large, and by many, to be negative. The Church has been accused of being judgemental, even discriminatory, towards people who are gay or lesbian. This is not surprising given that traditionally, the message has been one that begins, "Thou shall not" rather than "Thou are part of God's beautiful creation" and "Thou shall bring much to the Church".

On a flight back to Rome from the World Youth Day events in Brazil in 2013, Pope Francis reinforced the need to challenge this type of reaction to homosexuality, by asserting:

> *"If a person is gay and seeks God and has goodwill, who am I to judge them? They shouldn't be marginalised. The tendency [to homosexuality] is not the problem... They're our brothers." (2538)*

Pope Francis' pastoral approach to people who are gay is rooted in the following paragraph from *The Catechism of the Catholic Church*, which states that people who are gay "must be accepted with respect, compassion and sensitivity. Every sign of unjust discrimination in their regard should be avoided."

This does not mean that the Church's teaching on subjects like marriage and sexual relationships, as outlined here, is null and void, and should change. It means that we should strive to live according to the basic tenet – love my neighbour – seeing each person as an individual human being, not simply in terms of his or her sexuality.

This is an important point because all too often people are polarised into different groups (for example, "gay" or "straight"), which can dehumanise the individual and cause division.

So let's make it clear – the Catholic Church does not believe that people with a homosexual orientation should be persecuted in any way at all or that they should be socially excluded. Even though we hold to our teachings on subjects like marriage and sexuality, those who experience same-sex attraction are always welcome in our churches, schools, communities and lives. They too are the children of God.

> *"My dear people, let us love one another since love comes from God and everyone who loves is begotten by God and knows God."*
>
> **1 John 4:7**

Respecting the body

Your body is not just a vehicle for your soul to travel around in: it is an essential part of your sense of self. Your self is made in the image and likeness of God: that includes both the external as well as the internal. Therefore it is most important to honour our bodies and to act, as well as think, rightly.

The Church has always been at the forefront of this understanding of the beauty of the body, having at its centre the Body of Our Lord. Jesus is the Incarnation – God made flesh – and it is in his body that we encounter the great mystery of God. In the Eucharist we join our body to his, an intimate encounter that evokes the strongest feelings of love and belonging. And when we think of him crucified, it is again his physical body that we encounter – a naked and broken figure forcing us to confront his and our own humanity and vulnerability, forcing us to acknowledge the price willingly paid for our salvation. No shame or falseness – through the Body of Christ we are restored and made new again.

Contrast this with the "perfect body image" promoted in our culture, judging you only on appearance, selling an impossible idea of what you should look like. Think about how negative the message always is – you're too fat, your nose is too big or your skin is too greasy. Where is the freedom or individuality in this relentless message? Where is the kindness and compassion?

In all of this, who cares for and accepts YOU?

Consider the words of Sheila Cassidy, a doctor and author: "Those enduring great distress know that the cup cannot be taken away from them, but they value the presence of someone to share, however minimally, in their suffering – someone to watch with them during their agony. Jesus himself, when wrestling with his fear in the Garden of Olives, begged his disciples to stay with him; 'Could you not watch one hour with me?' "

How will you answer this question?

Our faith helps us navigate modern life. It provides a compass and guide, at the heart of which is love. Most of all, our relationship with Jesus teaches that every person is possessed of great beauty and that no one should be made to feel ugly or inadequate. In this respect and many others, the truth of our faith is one of complete liberation.

Science and faith: arguments for and against God

"Science can tell us how to do many things, but it cannot tell us what ought to be done."

Author unknown

Science and faith: arguments for and against God

Can you be considered "rational" while believing in the existence of God? Is it logical that all scientists ought to be atheists? Some people believe that one must choose to be a person of learning, science and reason, or choose to embrace religion, dogma and faith.

This view implies that religion and science are incompatible – they do not go together. But is this true? Can a person both accept what science teaches and engage in religious belief and practice? This is a complex question and deserves thoughtful consideration before a decision is made. By the end of this chapter, you should be able to make an informed judgement, as we look at the definition of "rational", apply it to the Catholic faith, and look at the relationship between religion and science, especially those scientific fields which seek to explain our existence.

What is rational?

A man and his friend, who happened to be an atheist, were debating the question: "Is it rational to believe in God?" They agreed that by "rational" they meant:

- **Self-consistent (not full of contradictions);**

- **does not fly in the face of what we already know and accept as true;**

- **is based on evidence.**

Unfortunately, they could not agree on what counted as "evidence".

The atheist insisted that only the results of scientific experiment counted as evidence. Since no scientific experiment can ever produce evidence of God, then it is irrational to believe in God.

The believer responded that the grandeur, beauty and complexity

of life is itself evidence of a creator behind it all. A work of art always has an author.

The atheist responded that yes, the universe is astonshingly beautiful, but theorectical physics can explain all of it without the need for a "God".

The believer responded, "Agreed. But an explanation is never a proof."

Is Catholicism rational?

The atheist was keen to continue the conversation. "Come on," he said, "your faith is itself nothing more than an 'explanation' rather than a 'proof'." The believer replied, "True, but I am not seeking to prove the existence of God to you."

The atheist presented another argument : "We agree that if Catholicism is rational then it must be self-consistent. There is nothing consistent in claiming that 'God is three and God is one'. Please explain how you can believe and still maintain you are being 'rational'."

The believer replied, "You are right. But you confuse 'inconsistent' with 'paradox'. Paradox might indicate inconsistency but it might also indicate truth is not always expressable in 'scientific' (forensic) language. For instance, how can self-preservation and sacrifical altruism be reconciled? And please don't start with 'memes' and 'selfish genes': even the scientific community has no time for them."

Both the atheist and the believer agreed on one thing: they were in for a long night...

Are faith and science compatible?

One of the great deceptions of the modern age is that faith and science are incompatible. This idea is completely untrue.

Faith is the name we give to our belief in God, and we can have faith for a whole variety of reasons. For example, we may have philosophical, emotional, rational, logical or entirely personal reasons for believing in God – none of which may necessarily be attached to a theory of science. That doesn't make them inadmissable.

That is what faith is like. As we saw in chapter three, to have faith is to fall in love – it is romantic, daring, exciting and life affirming. And we do not look to science for proof of these things. (Would you ask a scientist to define or even to prove to you that you are in love?) That's why, of course, we call it faith – faith in things unseen.

Science is the study of the material universe. It is, therefore, the study of "things". It doesn't matter if the things are very big (the universe itself) or very small (subatomic particles), they are still physical things.

Science, then, is simply the wrong tool to use for studying God, though not of course for studying God's creation. In fact, Catholics believe that the whole purpose of scientific enquiry is to better understand the universe created by God, and by doing so we better understand our place within the universe.

As human beings we are uniquely able to do this and for many centuries this was the underlying reason for all such enquiry – to glorify God through the study of God's creation. It is through science that we know we are here on this planet, which is a grain of sand on the shore of the universe. Yet from our tiny planet, we can look out to the heavens and give meaning to what we see. Why we are able to do this, and what the purpose of it might be, are not questions answerable by science alone.

"There were two ways of arriving at the truth. I decided to follow them both... Nothing in my working life, nothing I ever learned in my studies of either science or religion has ever caused me to change that opinion. I have no conflict to reconcile. Science has not shaken my faith in religion and religion has never caused me to question the conclusions I reached by scientific methods."

Monsignor Georges Lemaître

Did you know?

The Big Bang theory is widely considered the best explanation for how the universe came into being. However, few people know that it was developed in the late 1920s by a man of deep religious conviction. His name was Monsignor Georges Lemaître. Lemaître was a Belgian priest and scientist, who challenged ideas that set faith against reason, and science against the Catholic Church. His legacy extends beyond the field of science, to the nature of truth itself.

See pages 84-85 for more on Georges Lemaître.

Seven eminent Catholic scientists

1. Blaise Pascal (1623 – 1662)
Inventor of the adding machine, hydraulic press and the mathematical theory of probabilities

2. Georges Lemaître (1894 – 1966)
Father of the Big Bang theory

3. René Descartes (1596 – 1650)
Invented analytic geometry in the west and the laws of refraction

4. Gregor Mendel (1822 – 1884)
Founder of modern genetics

5. Nicolaus Copernicus (1473 – 1543)
First person to develop, scientifically, the view that the earth rotated around the sun

6. Louis Pasteur (1822 – 1895)
Founder of microbiology and creator of the first vaccine for rabies and anthrax

7. Alexander Fleming (1881 – 1955)
Discoverer of penicillin

If the Catholic Church were opposed to science, we would expect to find no or very few eminent Catholic scientists, but as it is, the list on the left is by no means exhaustive and can be used as evidence that there is no conflict between faith and science.

For the remainder of the chapter, we will look at two scientific theories, which have often been used to refute the existence of God, but which, as we will see, do no such thing.

Evolution: what do Catholics believe?

Jacques Monod, the Nobel Prize winning biologist, once famously remarked that a curious aspect of the theory of evolution is that everybody thinks they understand it, whereas very few people actually do.

So we might start by asking: What exactly is evolution?

Evolution is really the idea that life undergoes constant change, with one species capable, over time, of becoming another. Evolution depends on natural selection, which is the process whereby evolution happens. According to natural selection you need:

- life
- variation (for example, a gene mutation)
- inheritance (the variation must be passed down to the next generation)
- advantage (the individual of the species must in some way gain an advantage from the variation)

In essence, that's it.

For Catholics, the principal concern about evolution is whether it suggests that God is unnecessary. Does evolution do this? Well, it certainly provides us with a wonderfully elegant explanation of the variety of life on Earth. But it does not tell us where life came from or where the universe itself came from. So when we hear people confidently say that evolution disproves God or makes God's existence unnecessary, we can refute this because evolution only describes the physical development of life forms. It in no way undermines our belief in God as the author of life. God's are the physical laws that the evolutionary process follows.

For many Catholics, it is a revelation to learn that as far back as 1950 Pope Pius XII published an encyclical called *Humani Generis* (*On the Unity of the Human Race*), which discussed evolution. He said that evolution could not be expected to explain the origin of all things (which is clearly true).

Essentially, then, as Catholics, we have no problem believing that all life may have arisen through evolution, or indeed that it may be the mechanism by which God created our physical bodies (remember, however, that our souls were created directly by God). In fact, the astonishing beauty of the theory might make us grow in love towards God, recognising better how extraordinary the gift of life is, and how elegant and unified is God's plan of creation.

The Big Bang theory: fictional like the TV programme?

The science of cosmology (the study of the universe) tells us that the universe is likely to have originated in an event that we now call "the Big Bang", around 13.8 billion years ago.

The theory of the Big Bang (first called "the theory of the primeval atom") was originally advanced by a Catholic priest and scientist, Georges Lemaître, one of the geniuses of twentieth-century maths and physics, and a friend of Albert Einstein.

The Big Bang describes the event that brought into existence all matter and time (everything that is) following the laws of physics that govern our universe. Cosmology is all about understanding these laws – a journey of discovery that we are very far from completing.

So does the Big Bang "prove" God created the universe?

Even though it may point to a singular moment of "creation", we cannot say that it alone provides evidence of the existence of God. Lemaître himself resisted using his theory to do this, saying that the theory was an answer to a scientific question but not a religious one. For him, the existence of God remained the central mystery of his faith, neither proven nor disproven by science.

Do we know what caused the Big Bang to happen? This question is almost impossible to tackle, because it requires us to describe "existence" before anything existed. It is clear that we can hardly phrase such a question, let alone answer it. And it is not unreasonable to say that science can at best only offer speculation in this regard.

As Christians, we believe that everything was created by God. The details of how God created all things that exist is not that important. The point to remember is this: the Christian faith does not depend on an understanding of the laws of physics and we do not look to science to tell us everything we need to know about God.

Like Lemaître, we do not ask science to answer questions about God, because it cannot. Through faith and love, we grow closer to God and each other – and along the way we can give thanks for remarkable people like Lemaître and his contemporaries, men and women whose wisdom allows us to appreciate better the astonishing beauty of God's creation.

Catholic scientists throughout history have successfully reconciled their faith with science.

If a friend, who did not believe in God, challenged the compatibility of religion and science, how would you respond?

The Church: a force for good or evil?

"In this bright future you can't forget your past."

Bob Marley

The Church: a force for good or evil?

The Catholic Church seems to wear a permanent black eye these days. Under the weight of much criticism about members of the institution's hierarchy, some people are probably more convinced than ever that it's time for the Church to fade into history. But are recent revelations, as tragic and disturbing as they are, enough to overshadow two thousand years of positive influence on societies? Can the Catholic Church still be considered a force for good?

A force for evil?

Christians are called to be witnesses to the world – to live according to the values of the Gospel, and by doing so bring the peace and love of Jesus to all people. The Church has always held to this understanding, encouraging us to love others without requiring anything in return.

Unfortunately, in the Church's long history there have been times when the people who have been given authority to guide us in moral living have failed to live up to the high standards of our faith.

The main criticisms of the Catholic Church in recent years have fitted into five themes: (1) the unchristian way some Catholics behave, (2) the Church's perceived anti-science stance, (3) the promotion of sexual abstinence to curb the spread of HIV/AIDS, (4) the Church's view on homosexuality and (5) the sex abuse scandal. As we have seen throughout this book, much of the criticisms are unfair as they are based on misunderstandings of Church teachings and attitudes. However, the revelation about widespread sexual abuse by some priests over several decades is a truth that has left an indelible scar on the Church and those that it has hurt – making it the most damaging set of events to have occurred in the Catholic Church in modern times.

Sex abuse: not in our name

The familiar Gospel account of Jesus taking a child in his arms and receiving that child with love shows an attitude of care and concern for children. Jesus always seemed to find time for young people and he even told his disciples that unless they became like little children they would not enter the kingdom of heaven. He also warned his followers not to despise children or to cause them harm as children are valuable and are to be treated with love and care. Jesus' teachings have been faithfully followed by the Church, which has long believed that to receive a child in the name of Christ is to receive Christ himself.

However, in 2002 it became clear that a small, but significant, number of priests and lay members of religious orders in the Catholic Church had committed acts that were far from the message that Jesus preached about not causing harm to children. For five decades, from as far back as the 1950s, sexual abuse of minors by a priest, in particular, and the subsequent cover-up of his crime by his diocese or religious order were exposed as a repetitive pattern lived out in some areas throughout the world.

For thousands of men and women the abuse scandal is not just a newspaper story; rather, it is a painful and unforgettable part of their lives. They live, or try to, with the psychological and spiritual wounds inflicted on them as children by the people that they trusted.

Such shame forced the Church to pause for serious reflection: does the Church still have the credibility to bring Jesus' message of pure love and moral living to the world? Pope Francis has condemned members of the Church's hierarchy for hiding the abuse and said the Church must "weep and make reparation" for the "grave crimes" committed by clerics.

The Church agreed to a series of measures designed to protect children, and which also allow its priests – the majority of whom are excellent role models for children and young people – to continue their important ministry. The Church can never abandon its task of teaching, which is necessary to inform, inspire and bring people to Christ. But short of heaven, there will never be a Catholic golden age in which every minister of the Gospel follows the good out of deep conviction. Also, the Church is always going to suffer from those who rally against its message. But it is right that if it is to suffer, as Jesus predicted that it would, it should do so for the right reasons – for the sake of Jesus. To do good for souls, the Church must keep itself institutionally on point. That means it must not only teach, it must lead by example.

"Let the little children come to me, and do not stop them; for it is to such as these that the kingdom of heaven belongs."

Jesus

A force for good?

The Catholic Church and Catholic civilisation have contributed more to the world than any other body, organisation, nation or culture. This is a bold claim, no doubt, but in its two thousand year history Catholics have made outstanding contributions to every area of life.

The following is a tip-of-the-iceberg introduction to some of the things that the Church has given us. Much of the information draws from the work of Fr Marcus Holden and Fr Andrew Pinsent, who summarise in their book, *Lumen: The Catholic Gift to Civilisation*, the extraordinary enlightenment that Catholicism has brought to the world.

Science

Catholics are numbered among the most important scientists of all time. For example, as we have already seen, the most important theory of the origin of the universe – the Big Bang – was proposed by a Catholic priest, Monseigneur Georges Lemaître. The Augustinian monk Gregor Mendel founded the science of genetics. Cleric Nicolaus Copernicus first developed scientifically the view that the Earth rotated around the sun and Louis Pasteur created the first vaccines for rabies and anthrax.

More recently, Catholics constitute a good number of Nobel Laureates in physics, medicine and physiology, including Erwin Schrodinger, John Eccles and Alexis Carrel. How can the achievements of so many Catholics in science be reconciled with the idea that the Catholic Church opposes scientific knowledge and progress? It cannot!

Education

Perhaps the greatest single contribution to education to emerge from Catholic civilisation was the development of the university system.

Early Catholic universities include:

* Bologna
* Paris
* Oxford
* Salerno
* Vicenza
* Cambridge
* Salamanca
* Padua
* Naples
* Vercelli

By the middle of the fifteenth century there were over fifty universities in Europe. Many of them still show signs of their Catholic foundation, such as quadrangles modelled on monastic cloisters, gothic architecture and numerous chapels.

Starting from the sixth-century, Catholic Europe also developed what were later called grammar schools, with incalculable benefits for education. Today, it is estimated that church schools educate more than fifty million students worldwide.

Art

Several historians credit the Catholic Church for what they consider to be the brilliance and magnificence of Western art.

These works include:

* the great basilicas of Rome
* the work of Giotto, who initiated a realism in painting the Franciscan stations of the cross that helped to inspire three-dimensional art and drama
* The great works of the High Renaissance

The latter include the works of Blessed Fra Angelico (the patron saint of art) and the unrivalled works of Leonardo da Vinci, Raphael, Caravaggio, Michelangelo and Bernini. Many of the creations of these artists, such as the Sistine Chapel ceiling, are considered among the greatest works of art of all time.

Music

Musical genres that largely or wholly originated with Catholic civilisation include the hymn, the oratorio and the opera. Joseph Haydn, a devout Catholic, strongly shaped the development of the symphony and string quartet. Church patronage and liturgical forms shaped many works by Claudio Monteverdi, Antonio Vivaldi, Wolfgang Amadeus Mozart and Ludwig van Beethoven. The great Eighth Symphony of Mahler takes as its principal theme the ancient hymn of Pentecost, *Veni Creator Spiritus*.

Women

Contrary to popular prejudice, extraordinary and influential women have been one of the hallmarks of Catholic civilisation. The Catholic Church has honoured many women saints, including recent doctors of the Church, and nurtured great nuns, such as St Hilda, after whom St Hilda's College, Oxford, is named.

Pioneering Catholic women in political life include Eleanor of Aquitaine and the first Queen of England, Mary Tudor.

Catholic civilisation also produced many of the first women scientists and professors: Trotula of Salerno in the eleventh century, Dorotea Bucca, who held a chair in medicine at the University of Bologna, Elena Lucrezia Piscopia, the first woman to receive a doctor of philosophy degree, and Maria Agnesi, the first woman to become professor of mathematics, who was appointed by Pope Benedict XIV as early as 1750.

Dear Jesus, your Church has given so much to the world. Help me and all of those that form part of its body to give more. Motivate us to be your presence to minister to those that you came to help: those who are physically or spiritually weak, those with talents that need nurturing, and those who do not know your love.

I pray especially for your priests, your most holy ministers: give them a sincere faith, a burning love and true holiness which will increase in the course of their priestly lives. Amen.

Prayer

"Absolute unmixed
attention is prayer."

Simone Weil

Prayer

A saint was deep in prayer walking through the woods when an old man came up to him and asked what he was doing. "Praying," replied the saint, "but I have such difficulty with distractions." "I'm never distracted during prayer," said the man. The saint bet the man that he could not pray without being distracted. If he succeeded his prize would be the saint's horse. "Our Father who art in heaven," began the man, "does the saddle come with the horse?"

Prayer is the simplest and most natural way to communicate with God, yet why do so many of us find it difficult to do? Like the old man in the story, we can often become distracted during prayer. At other times we can be rather obsessive, churning out our prayers as a routine, rather like a dance in which a certain number of steps have to be included if we are to get it right. Miss a word or two and we get frustrated and begin all over again.

When we do manage to succeed in saying a good hearty prayer, it can sometimes feel as if we are simply talking to ourselves. No matter how hard we try to "feel" God's presence, we feel alone. This sense of isolation in prayer is called "spiritual aridity" – a feeling that God is not listening to us.

Be assured that if you are experiencing, or have experienced, any of the above, you are not alone. Blessed Mother Teresa of Kolkata wrote that for the last fifty years or so of her life she felt no presence of God whatsoever, neither in her heart nor in the Eucharist. That does not mean, though, that prayer was not an important part of her daily life.

Prayer helped Mother Teresa and helps us all to:

- grow spiritually
- grow mentally
- clarify our thoughts
- make better decisions
- better understand ourselves
- stay clear of bad things

Perhaps, most importantly, prayer allows us to admit our failures, our weaknesses and our limitations to the One who responds to human vulnerability with mercy and love.

Our Father who art in heaven, help me with my prayer...

When deciding to pray it does not matter if you recite existing prayers or pray "from the heart". God knows our thoughts even before we speak them. But if you find it spiritually helpful to pray using existing prayers then why not try the following:

At the start of term

Lord God,
As I start this new term, I ask you to be in everything that's going to happen: in every decision, in every challenge, in every victory, in everything I learn and in everything that I struggle with. Give me faith, give me perseverance, give me love for you and my neighbour. Amen.

At the start of the day

Lord God,
I'm not going to ask you for today to be predictable or easy. I'm not asking to be spared anything or given the easy option. But, as I start this new day, I ask you to stay with me and I ask you to get me through anything that may be difficult. Grant me the strength and the grace to do the right thing, and the ability to fix the things I don't get right. In everything today, give me happiness and joy, and help me to see your hand at work. Amen.

In sad times

Lord God,
When you walked on the earth, you
felt the same sadness that we feel. At
the moment, I'm feeling low. Things
aren't going my way and I'm finding
it hard to feel happy. You know what I
am going through and you know how
it can be healed, and so with an open
heart, I ask for your help. Help me to
remember that you are beside me,
that you care for me and that you hear
my prayer. Amen.

In happy times

Lord God,
Every good thing I have comes from
you. I thank you for all the amazing
things you have done for me, and for
the amazing things you will do in the
future. When things are going well,
may my joy reflect you to the people
around me. Amen.

Before exams, tests or deadlines

Lord God,
I'm about to start something important
and I'm at little worried. Guide me
through this with your caring hand
and help whatever comes out of it to
be fair and good. Whatever happens,
remind me that you have an amazing
and beautiful plan for my life, which
you won't allow to fail. Amen.

Who hasn't prayed before a big exam? There is nothing wrong in praying for a clear head and that you do your best, but prayer should not be used to replace study and hard work. God gave us an intellect and free will because God wants us to use both.

Before a holiday

Lord God,
Thank you for giving me this time to rest
and relax. May I make the best use of it.
May it be a time of peace and joy. May it
be a time to grow closer to you and closer
to those I love. May I come back ready
once again to do your work in the world.
Amen.

During times of stress

Lord God,
My heart isn't at peace at the moment
and I can't feel the joy you created me to
know as powerfully as I should. Too many
things are surrounding me and I'm finding
it difficult. I know that you will never leave
me and I know that you can always show
me the way through. Help me to find a
way back to peace, to love, and to being
the person you created me to be. Amen.

For the environment

Lord God,
You made a beautiful world and you
asked us to look after it. You ask us to care
for creation, just as you ask us to care for
our own lives and our own souls. Help us
to always treat the world around us with
care and respect. Bring strength to those
who work to rebuild damaged places and
bring a change of heart to those whose
work causes harm. Amen.

For my school, college or university

Lord God,
When you created us, you gave us
communities and people who care
for us. One of the most important
communities in my life is my [school,
college, university] and so I pray for
all of its members. Work in the hearts
of the teachers, the students, and
everyone else who supports and
cares for us. Give us success in what
we try to do – and in all things lead us
closer to one another and closer to
you. Amen.

For my family

Lord God,
I am so grateful to have a family that
loves me, cares for me and provides
for me. I ask you to watch over and
protect them. Keep us close to one
another and strong in our love for you.
Amen.

For the Church

Lord God,
Ever since Pentecost your Church has
worked for you throughout the world.
Sometimes things have been easy.
At other times, there has been great
suffering and persecution. Stay with
your Church as she does your work
in the world and help her work to be
fruitful. Amen.

The Lord's Prayer

Our Father, who art in heaven,
hallowed be thy name;
thy kingdom come;
thy will be done on earth as it is
*   in heaven.*
Give us this day our daily bread;
and forgive us our trespasses,
as we forgive those who
*   trespass against us;*
and lead us not into temptation,
but deliver us from evil.
Amen.

The Hail Mary

Hail Mary, full of grace,
the Lord is with thee.
blessed art thou among
*   women,*
and blessed is the fruit of thy
*   womb, Jesus.*
Holy Mary, Mother of God,
Pray for us sinners,
*   now and at the hour of*
*   our death.*
Amen.

Glory be

Glory be to the Father,
and to the Son,
and to the Holy Spirit.
As it was in the beginning,
is now, and ever shall be,
world without end.
Amen.

Why do Catholics pray to the saints?

Catholics recognise that Jesus is the only mediator between us and God the Father. This doesn't mean, however, that we cannot or should not ask our fellow Christians to pray with us and for us, including those Christians in heaven. The Bible shows us how the prayers of other people are helpful to us and it encourages us to ask for the prayers of others. For example, in the book of Genesis, God tells Abimelech that he is to return Sarah to Abraham and how because of Abraham's prayers Abimelech will be saved.

Last word

What now?

This book is longer than I wanted it to be and if you have read it then you have my thanks. I had planned something much shorter but as I began to write, more and more subjects and ideas kept appearing. I have managed to stop myself here, but I could have written a lot more – there is so much more to say.

It would be foolish to pretend that there are not deliberate and coordinated attempts being made to attack our Church – this book is really about how you, as young Catholics, might respond to those attacks.

No one can tell you what to think or what to do; you have free will and it is entirely up to you. My concern, though, is that a biased and one-sided media and public debate (which regularly puts the Church in the wrong) makes it difficult for anyone to form an objective opinion. That is why I wrote *The Survival Guide for Young Catholics*. I hope it has helped in some way to address the imbalance.

If you are a young Catholic trying to decide what to do next I do hope and pray that you will realise just what an extraordinary gift the Church is, to you and the world. Its people are not perfect, we have got things wrong and will continue to get things wrong – we are only human after all – but if our faith is true then we can have and want no other home. If you should stray, then I also hope that no matter how far you go you remember that in the Church you always have a loving spiritual home – your home.

But my real prayer is that you stay around, learn more about your faith and practise it with all your heart. Practise it openly and honestly. I also hope that you realise that it is you who can make a real contribution to the mission of the Church.

At the time of his ascension, Jesus said to his followers these remarkable words: "And behold I am with you always, yes to the end of time."

The strength these words contain is extraordinary. You are never alone, never unloved, never without your family in the Church. Remember them.

John Chater

Glossary

Abba
The Aramaic word for "father" that Jesus uses to address God the Father.

Abortion
Direct abortion is the ending of a pregnancy through the intentional killing of the unborn. The Church teaches that this is never justifiable under any circumstances.

Absolution
Freeing from guilt. Absolution takes place during the sacrament of reconciliation when the priest pardons sins in the name of God and the Church.

Actual Sin
See *sin*

Alb
A white liturgical garment.

Allegory
A story, poem or picture that can be interpreted to reveal a hidden meaning, typically a moral one.

Ambo
The reading stand where the scriptures are proclaimed during the liturgy.

Angel
A servant or messenger of God. Angels glorify God without ceasing, and watch over us every moment of our lives.

Annunciation
The angel Gabriel's announcement to Mary that she was to be the mother of Jesus Christ.

Apostolic
One of the four marks of the Church, along with one, holy and catholic. The Church is apostolic because she was founded on Jesus' twelve apostles. See *Marks of the Church*.

Ascension
The event forty days after the resurrection of Jesus Christ, when he was taken up to heaven.

Assisted suicide
The act of deliberately helping or encouraging another person to kill his or herself.

Assumption
The belief that God took Mary – body and soul – directly to heaven at the end of her life.

Atheism
The denial of God's existence.

Baptism
The first of the seven sacraments of the Church. Through baptism, people are cleansed of original sin and become united to Christ and to the Church. See *Sacrament*.

Bishop
One who has received the fullness of the sacrament of holy orders. A bishop usually takes care of the Church in a particular geographical area called a diocese. He is a sign of unity in his diocese and as a member of the College of Bishops, a sign of unity with the whole Church.

Blessing
A form of prayer in which we ask for God's loving care for someone, or some object or enterprise.

Catholic
Along with one, holy and apostolic, catholic is one of the four marks of the Church. Catholic means "universal". The Church reaches throughout the world to all people. See also *Marks of the Church*.

Celebrant
A person who celebrates a sacrament – for example, the priest who celebrates the Eucharist or the bishop who ordains a priest.

Charity
Working to meet people's needs out of love for God and neighbour. Charity, or love, is a theological virtue. See *Virtue*.

Chastity
The virtue of living your sexuality in a pure and healthy way, particularly by obeying the sixth and ninth commandments.

Chrism
Perfumed olive oil that has been consecrated. It is used for anointing in the sacraments of baptism, confirmation and holy orders (but not the deaconate). It is also used to consecrate a new church or altar.

Chrism Mass
The annual celebration during which a bishop blesses the oils to be used in his diocese during the coming year. This Mass usually takes place on Holy Thursday.

Christians
The name for followers of Jesus Christ.

Commandments, Ten
See *Ten Commandments*

Communion
The closest type of relationship shared among people, and between people and God.

Communion of saints
The whole community of now-living faithful people united with all those who have died but are alive with God in heaven.

Contrition
Sorrow for one's sins.

Conversion
A change of heart that turns us away from sin and towards God.

Covenant
A sacred agreement among people, or between God and human beings, where everyone vows to keep a promise.

Creation
God's action, through which all that exists has come into being.

Creed
A summary of Christian beliefs. The most familiar creeds are the Apostles' Creed and the Nicene Creed.

Deacon
Someone ordained to minister within the Church. Some men are ordained deacons as one stage of their preparation for eventual priesthood. Those who do not seek priesthood but commit to lifelong ministry to the Church are referred to as "permanent deacons".

Doctrine
Official teaching of the Church, based on God's revelation by and through Jesus Christ.

Ecumenism
The work of Catholics and other Christians, aimed at restoring unity among Christians.

Emmanuel
A name for Jesus that means "God with us".

Eucharist
A name for the Mass as a whole, or the consecrated bread and wine. Eucharist is based on a Greek term for "thanksgiving".

Eucharistic Prayer
The Church's great prayer of thanksgiving to the Father. It includes the consecration of the bread and wine.

Euthanasia
The act of deliberately ending a person's life.

Evangelise
To actively work to spread the Good News of Jesus Christ.

Faith
Accepting God's truth with our minds and having hope that it will guide our entire lives.

Free will
The gift from God that allows us to choose what we do. It is the basis for our moral responsibility.

Gifts of the Holy Spirit
Special gifts or graces we receive from God that help us live the way God wants us to live. The seven gifts of the Holy Spirit are wisdom, understanding, counsel (or right judgement), fortitude (or courage), knowledge, piety (or reverence) and fear of the Lord (or wonder and awe).

God the Father
The first person of the Holy Trinity.

Gospels
The Good News of God's revelation. The four Gospels – Matthew, Mark, Luke and John – tell us about the person, life, teachings, death and resurrection of Jesus Christ.

Grace
The gift of God's loving presence in our lives which enables us to share God's own divine life and love.

Heaven
The state of being in perfect friendship and unity with God for eternity.

Heaven and earth
A phrase that refers to everything that exists, the entire universe.

Hell
The state of being separated from God for ever.

Holy Communion
The sharing of Christ's body and blood in the liturgy.

Holy Spirit
The third person of the Holy Trinity.

Homosexuality
Sexual attraction to someone of one's own gender.

Human being
A living being made up of both a physical body and an immortal, spiritual soul. All human beings are created in God's image and likeness.

Idolatry
The worship of false gods or such things as money, possessions or popularity.

Immaculate conception
The belief that Mary was conceived without original sin.

Incarnation
The truth that Jesus Christ, the Son of God and the second person of the Holy Trinity, is both fully God and fully human.

Intercession
A form of prayer in which we ask for God's help for others.

Jesus Christ

Jesus is a Hebrew name that means "God saves". Christ comes from a Greek word used for "messiah" or "anointed one". The Son of God was named Jesus, signifying his role as saviour of the world. He was also called the Messiah or the Christ, signifying that he was the fulfilment of God's promises in the Old Testament. Jesus Christ is truly God and truly human and the second person of the Holy Trinity.

Judgement

An assessment of how we've lived our lives.

Justification

A process through which God restores our relationship with God after we have broken it through sin.

Kingdom of God

The reign of God which Jesus announced. It is characterised as a time of justice, peace and love. The seed or the beginning of the kingdom is present on earth right now. When the kingdom is fully realised in the future, God will rule over the hearts of all people.

Lectionary

The book that contains the readings that have been selected for proclamation during Mass throughout the year. All the readings are from the Bible.

Litany

A form of prayer, spoken or sung, which is addressed to God. It involves a dialogue between a leader and the people assembled. The people respond to each phrase said or sung by the leader with a constant refrain or acclamation.

Liturgy

The Church's official, public, communal prayer. It is God's work, in which the people of God participate. The Church's most important liturgy is the Eucharist (the Mass).

Logos

A Greek word that is translated as "word". It means "thought", "logic" or "meaning". Jesus is the Logos, because when we see Jesus and listen to him, we can begin to see the mind of God and understand God's mysterious plan.

Lord's Prayer

Another name for the Our Father, the prayer Jesus taught his disciples.

Magi

The wise men who, on discovering a strange star in the sky, travelled to Bethlehem to greet the newborn Jesus.

Magisterium

The teaching authority of the Church.

Marks of the Church
The four essential features or characteristics of the Church: one, holy, catholic and apostolic. See also *Apostolic; Catholic.*

Martyr
A person who voluntarily suffers death for the sake of his or her faith, or in defence of a virtue.

Messiah
Hebrew word for "anointed one". The equivalent Greek term is "Christos". Jesus is the Christ and the Messiah because he is the Anointed One.

Monotheistic
Describing the belief that there is only one God.

Mysteries
A term used by early Christians to refer to the sacraments.

Mystery
A truth that is so big and profound that no human being can completely know or understand it. We encounter mystery and enter into it.

Natural law
The God-given moral sense and voice of reason, which leads us to seek out what is good. It is called natural law because reason is part of human nature.

Original sin
See *Sin.*

Parables
Types of stories Jesus often used that draw on situations known to the listeners and surprise elements to teach about the kingdom of God.

Paschal mystery
The entire process of God's plan of salvation by which Christ saves us from sin and death through his passion, death, resurrection and ascension. We enter the Paschal Mystery by participating in the liturgy and being faithful followers of Christ.

Passion
Jesus' suffering and death.

Penance
A reference to the sacrament of penance (reconciliation), one of the seven sacraments of the Church. Through this sacrament sinners are reconciled with God and the Church.

Pentecost
Literally means "fiftieth day". It marks the day when the Holy Spirit came upon the apostles fifty days after the resurrection of Jesus.

Petition
A prayer form in which we ask God for forgiveness or for help with something.

Pope

The name for the leader of the Church. "Pope" comes from a word meaning "father". Sometimes the Pope is called the "Holy Father". He is the successor of St Peter, the first Pope and Bishop of Rome.

Reconcile

To restore relationships among ourselves and with God.

Reparation

Making up for the damage to property or the harm to another person as a result of one's sin.

Resurrection

The passage of Jesus through death to new life after he had been crucified.

Revelation

God's communication about God and God's plan for humanity. Throughout history God's revelation has been made known through creation, events and people, but mostly through Jesus Christ.

Sacrament

A visible sign and manifestation of God's grace. The seven sacraments are baptism, Eucharist, confirmation, reconciliation, anointing of the sick, matrimony and holy orders.

Salvation history

The pattern of events in human history through which God makes God's presence and saving actions known to us.

Sanctifying grace

God's free gift to us, which helps us to live in keeping with God's call.

Scriptures

A term for sacred writings. For Christians, the scriptures are the books in the Old and New Testaments that make up the Bible. They are the word of God.

Sin

It describes two separate realities: original sin and actual sin. Original sin is the sin by which the first humans disobeyed God, thereby losing their original holiness and becoming subject to death. Actual (or personal) sin is any deliberate offence in thought, word or deed, against the will of God.

Son of God

A title frequently given to Jesus Christ, the second person of the Holy Trinity.

Soul

The spiritual element that gives humans life and survives after death. The soul is created by God at the moment of our conception.

Stations of the cross
Images of Jesus' passion found on display in most Catholic churches.

Suicide
Taking one's own life.

Synoptic
"To see together". The Gospels of Matthew, Mark and Luke are called the synoptic Gospels due to their similarities.

Ten Commandments
The laws God gave Moses that guide human action. Jesus' command to love God and to love our neighbour is a summary of the Ten Commandments.

Thanksgiving
A form of prayer in which we express thanks and gratitude for the gifts God has given us.

Transubstantiation
The change that takes place when the bread and wine become the body and blood of Jesus Christ during Mass. Only the appearances (taste, smell and the like) of bread and wine remain.

Trinity
The central belief that there is one God in three divine persons: Father, Son and Holy Spirit.

Venerate
To show deep reverence for something sacred.

Virtues
Good habits that develop and help us to do the right thing. The four cardinal virtues are prudence, justice, temperance and fortitude. The three theological virtues are faith, hope and love (charity).

Vocation
The call from God to live a life of holiness. Some live out God's call as ordained priests, while others are called to marriage, to lives as members of religious communities, or to live as single people.